The Many wonders that Travel Through My Mind

The Many Wonders that Travel Through My Mind

FELICIA NOBLE WILLIAMS

iUniverse

THE MANY WONDERS THAT
TRAVEL THROUGH MY MIND

iUniverse books may be ordered through booksellers or by contacting:

iUniverse
1663 Liberty Drive
Bloomington, IN 47403
www.iuniverse.com
1-800-Authors (1-800-288-4677)

ISBN: 978-1-5320-8638-0 (sc)
ISBN: 978-1-5320-8639-7 (e)

Print information available on the last page.

iUniverse rev. date: 10/28/2019

A Prayer to God

As clouds try to darken my future, I
see the sun try to shine through.

As some people try to shut me down, I
stand strong with backing from you.

Like when I walk through the struggles
in my life I will have no fear.

For you are by my side and my
husband and family are near.

Sometimes I fight so hard for things I want
and when they don't come true I fall apart.

That's when you dust me off, and say "stand
strong, keep me and faith in your heart".

I don't know what you have in store for
me, but it must be something great.

Between the struggles I've been through
and the hurdles I have ran through, I'm
like a child who just can't wait.

So I'll keep going through my struggles, even though it can be hard, proving to the world that I am the right person for the job, just wait they'll see.

So the next time you walk in that big office, just keep in mind because it might just be me.

Felicia Noble-Williams

Can You Stand The Rain

Can you stop the tears that keep falling, while I try to make this hard decision?

Can we still be friends, even though I hurt your feelings, simply because it wasn't my intentions?

Is my love enough for you, or do you have to own me both body and soul?

Can you accept the fact that things have changed? That what was once hot has now turned cold?

I have loved you, like I have loved no other, and this is why this letter is so hard.

I know that this decision is hard to accept, but would you have preferred me sending a card?

I need to settle this confusion, because it weighs so heavily on my head.

This conflict has been tearing me apart, to the point it's hard to go to bed.

Don't hate me for making this decision. Just remember the good times that we shared.

How often do you find someone in life? Someone who really cared?

Felicia Noble-Williams

Conspiracy

Is this a conspiracy?

To finally get rid of me.

You have been trying so long.

Yet I still remain quite strong.

You try to undermind me every chance you get.

I'm not going anywhere. My mind is definitely set.

You talk about me, and make jokes about
me, trying to cost me my position.

Don't you know things you do, come back to
you even though that's not my intention.

You try to turn everybody against me,
thinking that you would win.

Don't you know there are people who fight for the
underdog and what you are doing is simply a sin.

Felicia Noble-Williams

Do You Know You're Special???

Do you know you're special? As special as they come.

Like a nice glass of wine or a sweet glass of rum.

Do you know you're special?, bringing
joy to the people you touch.

Spreading happiness with your smile,
that;s why I love you so much.

You always know what to do.

To make someone happy from blue.

You're a very special person, who
knows what everybody needs.

It's like watching a garden grow and
you planted all of the seeds.

You gave it what it needs, then sit
back and watch it grow.

People ask "what do you put in it?" you'll just
laugh and say "only I would ever know".

You are made up of so many things,
you have so many credentials

That's why you are who you are, that's
why you are so darn special.

Felicia Noble-Williams

Drama

You bring drama every place you go.

It's so real, your own family wish you didn't show.

Everytime you enter a room, people start to chatter.

Then when you come over, they start to scatter.

No one wants to be around you, you bring problems.

Only when you are gone, can
people begin to solve them.

Felicia Noble-Williams

Extreme

Do you always have to take things to the extreme?

Making a mountain out of a molehill,
messing up the team.

Why can't you leave well enough
alone, let go of your evil ways.

Give things time to heal, stop your
nasty moves, your nasty plays.

Always trying to find an opportunity to hit and run.

You are a horrible human being,
more deadly than a gun.

You torchure and harass people, making
people wish you were dead.

How do you live with yourself, when you're
alone? How do you sleep when you go to bed?

Felicia Noble-Williams

Happy Birthday

Today is your Birthday, I hope you have a great time.

We planned many things even lemonade with limes.

The invitations went out and the RSVP's came in.

Make sure your brother got his invite,
him not showing up would be a sin.

Put the liqour on the table and make
sure the shrimps are on ice.

Make sure the cake is ready, I better
call them even twice.

Put the sodas in the barrels, so the
guess can get to them.

Put the juices in the cooler, so they
can reach them, even little Tim.

Felicia Noble-Williams

Inseparable

As our hearts beat together I feel the
connection from you to me.

As the years pass by and still we are together,
this reminds me are we meant to be.

Through troubled times, through ups and
downs, we always stood together.

We are a team, through good and bad
times, through any kinds of weather.

If I had to sum it up to one word I would have
to say "incredible", because it's incredible
how we made it through the years.

For each passing day I think about the things we have
been through, and I thank God for no more tears.

Felicia Noble-Williams

Misunderstood

Just call me misunderstood.

Although I come from the hood.

That is not who I am.

I can be as quite as a lamb.

People often take advantage of my kindness.

They see it as a weakness

Don't believe the hype, I'm quite strong.

Don't let my personality fool you,
you would be very wrong.

I'm a very nice person, until you
change my perception.

I give people many chances, but
don't go along with deception.

Felicia Noble-Williams

My Black African King

My black brother, how do you do it?

Going through the struggles of life, like there's nothing to it.

You never seize to amaze me, how you stay so strong.

Fighting the ideas that people have about you, letting them see that they can be wrong.

You're mighty and strong, better than a $100 bill.

For when the wind blows in the park, you're like the tree that stands still.

You're a fighter by nature, with what life has put you through.

Don't let no-one put you down, tell them you're here to show and prove.

My gorgeous black man, stand correct and make your sister's proud,

Because when a sister sees nothing
but rain, it's you who can
make her see the sunshine through the clouds.

Felicia Noble-Williams

My Other Half

If someone would of told me tens years
later we would still be together.

I would of told them that they were crazy,
no way, no how and I know better.

But here we are, eleven years and three months later
with ten years of marriage. Where did the time go?

Through ups and downs and twist and
turns, but still we kept the flow.

We have accomplished more together than we did
apart and that's why I feel we were meant to be.

With two beautiful children and a marriage
that has held together there are more good
things to come, you just wait and see.

So I am writing you this poem to tell you
what our lives together has meant as we
travel along our harmonious path.

This is a token of my love on our anniversary day
to show and tell you why you are my other half.

Mrs. Felicia Noble-Williams

1 Man 1 Mind

1 man 1 mind.

1 soul you'll find.

Strong to the touch.

Never loved someone so much.

Unable to bend.

Heart strong like the wind.

1 family 1 block.

1 unit 1 rock.

Always stood fierce, love to set the trends.

Never stand alone, always had friends.

1 husband 1 wife.

2 children 1 life.

A family that plays together,

Stays together.

Love, Felicia Noble-Williams

Did You Know How Much I Loved You?

Did you know how much I loved you?

I think not, although many times
I wanted to tell you.

You were that father figure that I never had.

Like your words of wisdom always made me glad.

I hung on your words like they
were the words of the Lord.

I never got tired of hearing your
stories. I never got bored.

You were a man who was a wonderful
father with a fulfilling life.

A man with a variety of stories and an
exceptional also devoted wife.

Even near the end, you always took time for me.

To ask me about my mother, always
taking the focus off of thee.

You might not of been my real father,
but you was the closest thing I had.

That is why you leaving this earth
have made me very sad.

So I ask you "Pop", "did you know how much
I loved you?" for I hope you did because I
tried to let it show.

For if you didn't, I'm telling you now that I
loved you more with each passing day and
more than you could ever know.

Your Daughter-in-Law,
Felicia Noble-Williams

Question??????

What makes a person turn from
good to bad or bad to good?

What makes a person move from where
they lived, or stay in the hood?

What makes a poor person live like they're rich
and a rich person live like they're poor?

What makes a person live in a terrible place
with expensive furniture and a person live in a
beautiful place while sleeping on the floor?

What makes a person get involved
versus walking or looking away?

What makes a person run for the hills versus
stand your ground, fight, and stay?

Felicia Noble-Williams

Someone Special

Don't let my looks fool you, deep down I'm really sad.

To think you would throw away three years
with that girl, makes me very mad.

She's a beautiful woman with no children,
who's adored by your mama.

No you rather throw it all away for
some baby-mama-drama.

Are you crazy??? to risk it all? What do
you think, this is some kind of sport.

Taking a chance, with an older woman with
children, who probably sue you for child support.

Haven't you been to court enough? Are
you trying to break a record for being
in court for the stupidest things?

When you have a beautiful young woman, who loves
you very much, waiting for you to give her that ring.

Felicia Noble-Williams

The Empowered Woman

The empowered woman fights for what she has.

Never accepting no and never letting anything pass.

Conquering all the challenges that face.

This woman means business; she
knows the thrown is her place.

She's unstoppable, unbreakable,
this woman will not bend.

Always helping anyone who needs her,
always lending an ear to a friend.

She never stands on the side she
has to be on the front line.

Just her presence in the room sends
a chill down anyones spine.

A woman who walks so soft, but who
you could sense a mile away.

A woman so quite, yet I can hear
her voice even today.

No matter how many hurdles she came across she
always stood up to them, never stayed seated.

So in my eyes Henrietta your not
dead, just retired undefeated.

Felicia Noble-Williams

The Evil Within

How can you stop the evil within?

When everything in your heart
tells you it's a terrible sin.

You try to surpress it, and try to walk away.

But the pain in your heart always convince it to stay.

You pray on it and ask God to help you forgive.

But the anger in your heart saids
"You need me to live."

The burning in your heart helps
you to keep up the fight.

It helps keep you safe until God brings you light.

Felicia Noble-Williams

"The Life Of The Party"
You Are Sexy

Look, He has arrived, Biggie is finally here.

Everybody rushes over. He walks in
the room, they start to cheer.

The party can finally start, the man
of the hour is about to finally arrive.

Better get to your seats quick for it's about to be live.

Your big and strong, you dress to a "T".

The girls go wild, your boys hold you
down, it's about you cant you see.

Your smile lights up the room. It's
like Christmas all year.

Spreading gifts to the girls going out with the
boys, everybody's down with the cheer.

Felicia Noble-Williams

The Mirror

When you look in the mirror, what do you see?

The ugliness inside of you or the beauty
outside of you, that's not for me.

Do you see the evilness that you possess
or the evil things you do?

No because you say "It's all about me"
meaning it's all about you.

You do know what goes around comes back
around, and it can affect your family as well.

Just for you to keep things going you
probably thinking "that's swell".

So don't question why you keep getting sick or your
family has problems, don't even ask your mama.

Because as long as you keep doing people
dirty, your life will always have drama.

Felicia Noble-Williams

The unspoken word

There are rules and regulations
to everything you follow.

You can only live for today, for no
one is promised tomorrow.

Even in life there are things you
should automatically know.

Things that should not be said.
things not meant for show.

How many meetings do you need
to get the picture right?

How many times are you gonig to do
this before it leads into a fight?

Why cant you just leave well-enough alone?

Ugly might be skin deep, but evil
is way down to the bone.

Why must you torchure people to
make yourself feel good?

Some people leave the ghetto, but
mentally stay in the hood.

Felicia Noble-Williams

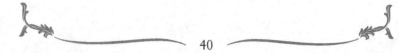

The Weekend

Everything happens on the weekend.
The weekend is the best.

You can go somewhere to dress casual
or somewhere to dress to impress.

The weekend is to relax or to party,

You can eat light, or eat hearty.

You can go out to wine and dine or go out to the club.

You can go to a nice restaurant or out to the pub.

You can go for the whole weekend or just for the day.

You can go out for a couple of hours
or get a hotel and stay.

You could relax all day and party all night.

It could be a busy weekend or just keep it light.

Felicia Noble-Williams

What Valentine's Day Means to Me

Valentine's day means being in love,
Holding hands, walking in the park.

Being with your partner all day long
and staying up way after dark.

Eating breakfast in bed with juice on
one side and a rose on the other.

In the afternoon getting cupid
tattoos saying, "for my lover."

Spending the evening getting dressed
up to go to a nice play.

Then finish the night off with a romantic dinner
That tells your partner he won't
be leaving, "not today."

A candlelight dinner in an elegant
setting, would be just right.

Then watch the movie "Sleepless in Seattle"
And cuddle through the night.

FeliciaNoble Williams

work

Work hard, play hard, live life to the fulliest.

Work hard, play hard, take care of your business.

Work hard to take care of your bills
and everyone in your family.

Work hard to send your kids to school
to go to that special academy.

Work hard to save up money to buy that special car.

Work hard to get that apartment so you don't live far.

Work hard to open a bank account
that's only in your name.

Work hard to get that promotion,
sometimes it's like a game.

Work hard to go on that trip that
you always wanted to do.

Work hard to do all the things that
life has in store for you.

Felicia Noble-Williams

You Think It's Easy Being Me???

You think it's easy being me?

Try to walk four blocks in my shoes
and you would want to be free.

My life is like a well oiled machine, needing
to be maintained to get through the day.

No room for errors, no room for
things to get in my way.

I have to stay focused on the bigger
picture to keep things alive.

This is the story of my life. It's not no nine to five.

I have many people depending
on me, so I can not fail.

It's that deep, It's that serious, trying to
prevent people from going to jail.

Felicia Noble-Williams

You're A Diamond

You're a diamond and you know it.

The whole world can see and you show it.

Your face, your hair, your style, your flair.

Like a diamond you set off a glare.

The whole world sees you and they stop and stare.

Your picture people want it.

You're beautiful, people love when you flaunt it.

Men and women love you.

Your friends admire you.

Your family adores you.

Your parents Princess supports you.

Felicia Noble-Williams

Printed in the United States
By Bookmasters